PICKLE HILL PRIMARY
WHERE ANYTHING CAN HAPPEN

MRS PARROT'S RAINFOREST

LESSONS

Michael Cox

illustrated by
Kelly Waldek

KT-385-271

SCHOLASTIC

To Ted Cox

(3rd April 1923 – 10th November 2002)

Scholastic Children's Books,
Commonwealth House, 1–19 New Oxford Street,
London WC1A 1NU, UK

A division of Scholastic Ltd
London ~ New York ~ Toronto ~ Sydney ~ Auckland
Mexico City ~ New Delhi ~ Hong Kong

Published in the UK by Scholastic Ltd, 2003

Text copyright © Michael Cox, 2003
Illustrations copyright © Kelly Waldek, 2003

All rights reserved

ISBN 0 439 97813 0

Printed by Cox & Wyman Ltd, Reading, Berks

2 4 6 8 10 9 7 5 3 1

The right of Michael Cox and Kelly Waldek to be identified as the author
and illustrator of this work respectively has been asserted by them in
accordance with the Copyright, Designs and Patents Act, 1988.

This book is sold subject to the condition that it shall not, by way of trade
or otherwise be lent, resold, hired out, or otherwise circulated without the
publisher's prior consent in any form of binding or cover other than that in
which it is published and without a similar condition, including this
condition, being imposed on the subsequent purchaser.

Contents

WELCOME TO

PICKLE HILL PRIMARY

Hi! My name's Liam O'Brady and I go to Pickle Hill Primary, which is not like any other school on the planet. I suppose it's our teachers who make Pickle Hill so weird. Every one of them has a really amazing (and completely brilliant!) way of teaching their subject. And they really like to surprise us.

Take Mrs Parrot! You've got to keep an eye on her, 'cos you never know what she's going to get up to next! One minute you might be sitting on the class rug waiting for a story, and the next you're sitting on the same rug, orbiting the earth!

If you're still not sure what I mean, why don't you join me and the rest of 5M for Mrs Parrot's unforgettable rainforest lessons!

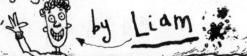 by Liam

5

PICKLE HILL PRIMARY

Teacher's name: Mrs Parrot
(known to her friends as 'Polly')

Age: 47 (but she says she's 37)

Appearance: Dyed sticky-up hair
and large nose

Subject: Geography

Favourite topic: Rainforests

Quirks, tics or odd
behaviour:

Flaps her arms a
lot and hops around
the classroom when
she gets excited.

Information
supplied by:
Liam O'Brady. Class 5M

Raining bats and frogs

It was absolutely throwing it down when Mrs Parrot came rushing into our classroom last Thursday morning.

"Phew!" she said, looking at her dripping waterproofs. "Talk about wet! It's raining bats and frogs out there!"

"Er, Mrs Parrot?" said Charlotte Edwards. "I think you've got it wrong. You're supposed to say it's raining *cats and dogs*."

Mrs Parrot flapped her arms excitedly, and said, "No I'm not! Not today, anyway." Then she opened her left hand and said, "Look!"

Sitting on her palm was a large, shiny, red

8

tomato. At least, we thought it was a tomato. But then it began to grow! And a moment later it opened its mouth and croaked!

"Yikes!" gasped Brian Butler. "It's a frog!"

"Yes," said Mrs Parrot. "It's a tomato frog."

"But ... but ... what's it doing at Pickle Hill?" said Daniel Mapson. "I thought you only got frogs like that in places like –"

"RAINFORESTS!" screeched Mrs Parrot, making us all nearly fall off our chairs. "Exactly! And *they're* what we're going to be learning about! All the different types of rainforests of the world! Where you also find these."

And then she opened her right hand. Sitting on her palm was a bat.

"This," said Mrs Parrot, "is a spear-nosed, long-tongued bat found in the Amazon jungle!

When it's not drinking nectar from the flowers of banana trees, it's chasing the mice, birds and other smaller bats it likes to eat."

"We'll be seeing stacks more amazing creatures later on," Mrs Parrot said, closing her palms. She took a deep breath, opened them again, and the little creatures were gone. Then she said, "But before we do any of that, we'd better make sure that everyone knows exactly what a rainforest is!"

"I know!" said Laxmi Sharma. "It's a tropical forest that gets really heavy rainfall."

"And it's hot and steamy," said Zoe Thompson. "With lots and lots of different sorts of trees."

"Heavy rainfall! Hot and steamy! Lots of trees!" repeated Mrs Parrot, hopping wildly around the classroom. "Yes! Yes! Put simply, that's more or less it! Well done, both of you! And it's thought that, even though the rainforests only make up five per cent of the earth's surface, more than half of all the plants and land creatures in the world live in them!"

"Cripes! Rainforests must be absolutely bursting with wildlife!" said Brian.

"They are!" said Mrs Parrot. "And Laxmi, you're right about the rain! Rainforests get lots and lots of it. They get between 2 and 12 metres a year on average, while here at Pickle Hill we only get about half a metre! Hard to believe on a day like today, though."

Mrs Parrot looked at the enormous raindrops rolling down our windows. Then she tottered over to the doors that lead to our wildlife garden and looked out. Our school playing field and the garden were now completely hidden by the rain!

"OK! I think it's easing off, now!" said Mrs Parrot with a smile.

It stopped raining suddenly, and we couldn't believe our eyes. Outside was a tangle of branches, creepers and enormous tree trunks ... all dripping wet.

"OK, class!" said Mrs Parrot. "Grab your waterproofs and come outside!"

"Ha!" cried Daniel, as we stepped out. "We've got a jungle in a jiffy!"

"How convenient!" said Mrs Parrot. "Now we need our thermometer and classroom clock."

"I'll get them!" said Brian.

A few seconds later he was back.

"Right, we'll begin!" said Mrs Parrot, and the clock's hands whizzed to 6 a.m.

13

14

"So that's the rainforest forecast for today," said Mrs Parrot. "And in many rainforests, that's more or less what happens *every* day. There's almost no need for a weather forecast because you can just about guarantee that this is the weather you'll get all year round!"

"Now I can see why it's called the *rain* forest," said Charlotte, as we all trooped back into our classroom.

"Yes!" said Mrs Parrot. "All those plants and trees depend on that daily downpour for their survival. So, in a way, the rain creates the rainforest!"

"And the rainforests create the rain!" said a voice in the art corner.

Bud Green

We all turned to see who'd spoken but the only living thing in the art corner was our enormous Swiss cheese plant. As we stared at it, we suddenly noticed that its leaves were quivering and that one of the holes in them had turned mouth-shaped! And a second later the mouth spoke!

HI! THE NAME'S BUD... BUD GREEN. I WANT TO TELL YOU ALL ABOUT THE IMPORTANT STUFF US RAINFOREST PLANTS DO!

Zoe was the first to recover from her shock. But Zoe's like that, cool and calm, whatever the situation.

"Er … Bud," she said. "I thought you were from Switzerland!"

"As if!" yelled Bud. "I'm only called *Swiss* because these holes in my leaves make me look like a piece of Swiss cheese! I'm originally from Central America – a genuine rainforest plant."

"Yes! And so am I!" said another voice. It came from the little African violet on Mrs Parrot's desk!

"And me!" said the busy Lizzie plant on the bookshelf.

Suddenly there were plants talking all over the place.

"Mrs Parrot," said Brian. "Lots of our classroom plants are saying they're from the rainforest. But I thought they all came from the garden centre!"

"They did," said Mrs Parrot. "But that's not the whole story. You see, back in the nineteenth century, thousands of their great (times-ever-so-many) grandparents were taken from the rainforests because rich Europeans wanted unusual plants to impress their posh friends. Now people are used to having them around, and don't realize that they came from the rainforest in the first place. You've probably got rainforest plants in your own homes."

Laxmi, who's always incredibly polite and well behaved, put her hand up and said, "Er, excuse me, sir – I mean, Mr Bud – do the plants in the rainforests really create its rain?"

"They sure do!" said Bud. "Check it out if you don't believe me!"

"And that's not *all* we do!" said Bud. "If you want to know about our most *importanto*, *numero uno* job we need to talk *energy*, don't we Polly?"

"Sure do, Bud!" said Mrs Parrot. "Energy's the stuff we all need to live. Humans, plants and every other living creature on the planet need it! Without it, we're nothing!"

Bud suddenly waved one of his leaves right in front of Kelly Niblett's face, then said, "So kid! Where do we all get this energy from?"

"Er ... energy drinks?" said Kelly, looking completely terrified.

"The sun!" barked Bud.

"That's right," said Mrs Parrot. "The energy that keeps *all* of us alive, travels all the way from the sun to the earth in the form of heat and light."

"But once it gets here it has to be *captured* and *stored*!" said Bud. "And you animal saddos aren't much good at doing that. Not like us super-smart green plants! *We* can package and *save* that energy! And if we didn't do that, you guys would just be heaps of dry bones! In fact, all living things are *made* from plants!"

Bud waggled his leaves, then said, "In every one of these here leaves of mine there's green stuff called chlorophyll."

"Is that why you're so green?" said Laxmi.

"Yes," said Bud. "Gorgeous, aren't I? And it's my chlorophyll that traps the light energy from the sun. I change that light energy into *stored* energy using photosynthesis."

"A photo of whose sis?" said Daniel.

"I said *photosynthesis*, cloth ears!" cried Bud. "You look like you've got a brain somewhere between those big ears of yours. So, why don't you find out how it works!"

"What ... my *brain*!" said Daniel, looking confused.

"No, dimwit!" said Bud. "Photo-flipping-synthesis!"

"And photosynthesis isn't all we do!" said Bud, tapping Kelly on the shoulder with one of his leaves. "You animals and us plants have a *very* special relationship!"

"The thing is," said Bud. "Not only are we making lots of scrummy energy-giving nosh for you, but we're also recycling your waste breath, which contains the carbon dioxide we need. And of course, the waste product from our photosynthesis is..."

"Oxygen!" yelled Simon "Three Brains" Sidworth, who's just about the cleverest kid in our class.

"Which *we* all need for survival!" said Laxmi, who's almost as smart as "Three Brains" (and definitely much better looking).

"Quick thinking, you kids!" said Bud. "Yes! We're putting *your* waste products to good use and you're putting *our* waste products to good use! It's all beautifully worked out."

"Yes! Beautifully worked out!" cried Mrs Parrot, flapping her arms excitedly.

"And it's not just the waste products from your lungs we're converting and storing," said Bud. "It's all that other muck you chuck out from your cities and cars. The rainforests often act as massive storehouses for the stinky stuff given off by factories and traffic and all the other mega-polluting man-made things of the twenty-first century."

HE'S RIGHT! THE AMAZON RAINFOREST CONTRIBUTES TO OUR PLANET'S OXYGEN SUPPLY BY CONTINUOUSLY CHANGING CARBON DIOXIDE INTO OXYGEN.

"We're amongst the most environmentally friendly things on earth!" said Bud "We're about as *green* as you can get!"

"So does that mean that even our little wildlife garden is helping to keep the air clean?" said Laxmi.

"Definitely," said Bud. "Not to mention all the trees and shrubs on your playing field. Every little helps, you know. It's just a pity that the maniac with the shears and the chain-saw is forever trimming and chopping them."

"Oh, you mean Slasher Simpson, our school gardener!" laughed Daniel.

"Daniel!" said Mrs Parrot. "It's Mr Simpson to you! But, yes! I do agree. That man is a menace. Put a chain-saw in his hands and he turns into Attila the Lumberjack!"

"There are far too many 'Slashers' in this world," said Bud. "Why they can't just leave us plants and trees to get on with our jobs is beyond me."

"I know just what you mean, Bud!" said Mrs Parrot. Then she clapped her hands and said, "Now children! For homework, some of you can ferret out a few more facts about the fascinating plants and trees that come from the rainforest! There are thousands to choose from."

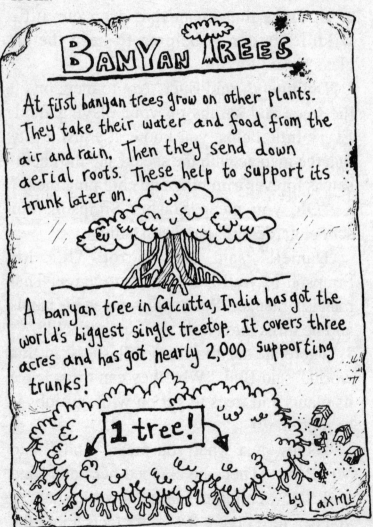

BaNYaN TReeS

At first banyan trees grow on other plants. They take their water and food from the air and rain. Then they send down aerial roots. These help to support its trunk later on.

A banyan tree in Calcutta, India has got the world's biggest single treetop. It covers three acres and has got nearly 2,000 supporting trunks!

1 tree!

by Laxmi

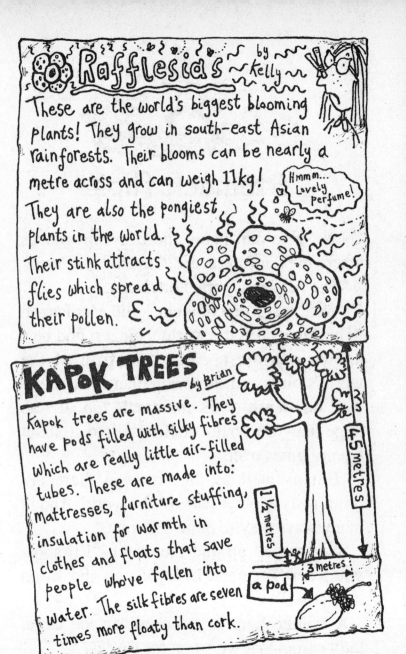

Rafflesias
by Kelly

These are the world's biggest blooming plants! They grow in south-east Asian rainforests. Their blooms can be nearly a metre across and can weigh 11kg!

They are also the pongiest plants in the world. Their stink attracts flies which spread their pollen.

Hmmm... Lovely perfume!

KAPOK TREES
by Brian

Kapok trees are massive. They have pods filled with silky fibres which are really little air-filled tubes. These are made into: mattresses, furniture stuffing, insulation for warmth in clothes and floats that save people who've fallen into water. The silk fibres are seven times more floaty than cork.

45 metres

1½ metres

3 metres

a pod

Stomach flips

"Now, who can name the different places where the rainforests are?" asked Mrs Parrot.

"The Amazon!" cried out Kelly.

"Well, that's one of them," said Mrs Parrot. "The Amazon is the world's biggest and best known rainforest. About one-fifth of the world's birds and flowering plants live there. And one-tenth of its mammals *too*. It's so huge that you could fit Britain into it about twenty times over.

"But as well as the Amazon there are rainforests in other parts of the world. And in many ways they're quite different."

She jumped up and then said, "I'll show you where they are. Everyone go and sit on the carpet."

A minute later we were all on the large, tatty carpet that we sit on for stories.

Suddenly, we heard the most incredibly loud "Whooooooooosh!" and felt the wind whistling past our ears, as our stomachs did that thing they do when you're going up on a roller-coaster. And then we were somewhere that definitely *wasn't* Pickle Hill Primary!

"Er, Mrs Parrot," said Brian. "Where are we?"

"We're cruising, dear," said Mrs Parrot, "at about 10,000 metres. Quite a remarkable feat for a carpet of this age, but then again it is a *very* remarkable carpet. That big round thing you can see below you is the earth."

"If you look very carefully, you'll notice that all of the world's rainforests are labelled to help you identify them!"

"Now, has anyone spotted anything about the position of the rainforests on our planet?" said Mrs Parrot.

"Yes," said Zoe. "They're all around the middle part."

"Well done, Zoe. That's right!" said Mrs Parrot. "They're all near the imaginary line known as the equator, in the region we call the tropics. This means all the rainforests are hot and get lots and lots of rain and are always warm and wet."

"Now! I think it's time to pay a swift flying visit to the rainforests!" continued Mrs Parrot.

"But there's one more important thing you should know. As well as rainforests occurring in different bits of the world, there are also different *types* of rainforest. And I think writing about them would make an excellent homework topic! OK! Down we go!"

The next moment, our stomachs did that thing they do when you're going *down* on a roller-coaster and we saw that we were plummeting towards the south-east Asian rainforests.

We left Asia and paid a flying visit to an Australian rainforest!

Then we zoomed off to Africa....

AFRICA'S RAINFORESTS DON'T HAVE AS MANY SPECIES OF ANIMALS AND PLANTS AS OTHER FORESTS BECAUSE LOTS OF THEM DIED OUT WHEN AFRICA'S CLIMATE GOT DRIER DURING THE LAST ICE AGE, ABOUT 15,000 YEARS AGO. BUT THEY'RE STILL AMAZING PLACES!

ONCE UPON A TIME NEW GUINEA, AUSTRALIA AND NEW ZEALAND WERE ALL ONE MASSIVE CONTINENT COVERED IN RAINFOREST. THE BIGGEST AUSTRALASIAN FORESTS ARE IN NEW GUINEA AND THE SMALLEST ARE HERE IN AUSTRALIA.

And finally we carpeted off to the South and Central American rainforests…

Two seconds later we felt a gentle bump as our trusty old carpet landed back in the book corner!

"That *was* fun, wasn't it!" said Mrs Parrot.

"Absolutely ace!" I said. "But I wish we could have had a closer look at the Amazon rainforest. I'd love to go there."

"Me too!" said Kelly.

"Don't worry, children," said Mrs Parrot. "We will visit the Amazon rainforest, but not on a tatty old carpet."

"How then?" said Daniel.

"Wait until next lesson – then I'll show you!" said Mrs Parrot.

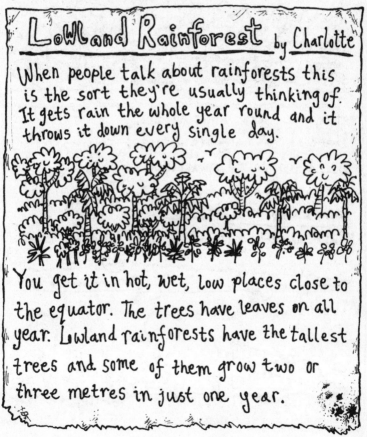

Lowland Rainforest by Charlotte

When people talk about rainforests this is the sort they're usually thinking of. It gets rain the whole year round and it throws it down every single day.

You get it in hot, wet, low places close to the equator. The trees have leaves on all year. Lowland rainforests have the tallest trees and some of them grow two or three metres in just one year.

MANGROVE FORESTS by Laxmi

The seashores of some countries like Bangladesh in Asia have mangrove forests. The roots of mangrove trees look like stilts. They hold the coast mud together and stop it being clobbered away by stormy seas.

Here are some amazing things you find in Bangladesh mangrove forests:

- Weird fish called mudskippers which crawl across the land and climb trees!

- Eight-metre-long crocodiles which kill young tigers.

- Tigers which swim a lot.

Cloud Forests by Brian

Cloud forests grow on tropical mountains above 900 metres. They are misty a lot of the time. There are cloud forests in the Congo in Africa where there are lots of gorillas. The trees in them are low and twisty with moss and ferns and lichens growing on them which look like beards. I don't think I'd like to go to it because you never know what you might bump into!

At night it can be freezing cold in cloud forests even though they are tropical.

MONSOON FORESTS

by kelly

These are tropical forests which don't get rain for three months of the year. The trees lose their leaves when it's dry but then they grow new ones. When the monsoon rains come it really <u>CHUCKS</u> it down and the forests often flood.

Spiny anteaters live in Australian rainforests and eat ants and worms. They carry their babies in a pouch but when the babies grow their spines they have to get out. Ouch!

These are the sort of forests where teak grows — a really valuable tree used in lots of furniture.

Tall storeys

The next lesson Mrs Parrot flung open the door to our stockroom. "So!" she said proudly. "What do you think to *that* then?"

In the space where the science cupboard normally stands was one of the biggest, shiniest glass lifts any of us had ever seen!

"May I offer you all a *lift*!" laughed Mrs Parrot. She pushed a button, the lift doors slid open and we all piled in. On the control panel inside there was a guide to the different levels, just like in big department stores. Except this was for the different storeys of the rainforest!

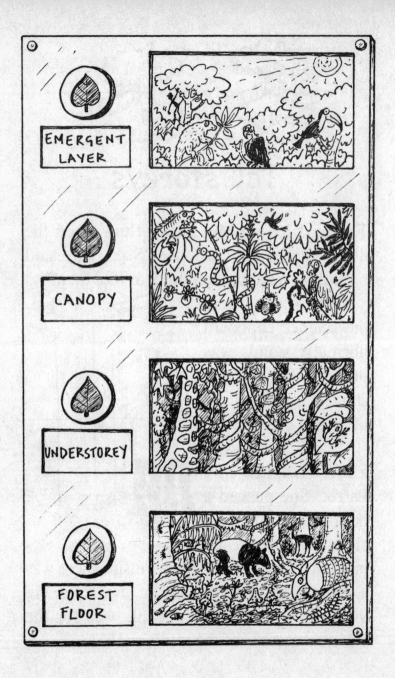

EMERGENT
LAYER

CANOPY

UNDERSTOREY

FOREST
FLOOR

"We'll give the forest floor a miss for now," said Mrs Parrot. "Let's go to one of the world's last unexplored frontiers!"

"Wow!" said Simon. "Where's that then?"

"The rainforest canopy, of course!" said Mrs Parrot. "That and the deepest oceans floors are about the only places on earth that still hold secrets unknown to humankind. Both are home to masses of species that haven't been seen by anyone. And on the way up we'll be seeing tonnes more interesting stuff. OK, lift *off*!"

And up we went!

We pressed our noses to the glass so that we didn't miss a single thing – Mrs Parrot included!

The first things we noticed were the masses of trees that surrounded our lift. Loads of trees had great tangles of vines and creepers dangling from them, like a giant green web. And we hadn't been going up long when the heat hit us. And the higher it went the more we sweated!

"This is the understorey," said Mrs Parrot. "It's gloomy like this because the canopy cuts out most of the sunshine. Young plants that don't need much light grow here."

As well as getting hotter all the time, we now also began to notice something else. Lots of noises! At first they were quite faint, but the higher we went, the louder they became. Soon, the air was filled with buzzing, twittering and howling!

Then, as the glass lift climbed even higher, we began to see flashes of movement and colour in the trees around us. Before long, we were spotting huge swarms of insects buzzing around enormous, brightly coloured flowers and flocks of red and yellow parrots flapping noisily from tree to tree.

"I think we'll pause for a moment and admire the scenery," said Mrs Parrot. She pressed the STOP button and the lift came to a halt.

"Wow, look!" said Brian. "*That* is amazing!"

He was pointing at two birds with enormous, coloured beaks. They were sitting a few metres apart from each other on a branch and were tossing some sort of fruit backwards and forwards.

"They're toucans," called Mrs Parrot. "Fruit throwing is their way of showing that they're feeling playful!"

"So!" cried Daniel. "Toucan ... play at that game. Ha ha ha!"

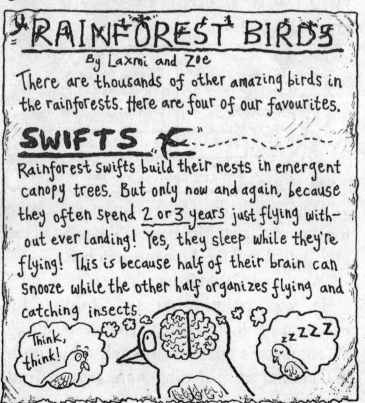

RAINFOREST BIRDS
By Laxmi and Zoe

There are thousands of other amazing birds in the rainforests. Here are four of our favourites.

SWIFTS

Rainforest swifts build their nests in emergent canopy trees. But only now and again, because they often spend <u>2 or 3 years</u> just flying without ever landing! Yes, they sleep while they're flying! This is because half of their brain can snooze while the other half organizes flying and catching insects

Think, think!

zzZZZ

HORNBILLS

Big and noisy birds which live in African and Asian rainforests. Female Rhinoceros hornbills lay their eggs in hollow trees after blocking themselves in with mud! They leave a tiny opening for the male to post fruit, snakes, lizards, and insects to her and her babies.

If something happens to the male, the female and babies can die from being blocked in and getting no food but sometimes another male without a mate comes along and starts feeding them.

OROPENDULAS

These live in the rainforests of South America and are really crafty. They always make their own nests near stinging bee, wasp, or ant nests. This makes their enemies think twice about attacking them.

nest

PARROTS

There are 315 different sorts of parrots in the world.

Bright colours

Loud call:
Squawk squawk!

Powerful beak:
for cracking hard shells and grinding food, and useful for climbing.

Feet: two toes facing forwards, two facing backwards.

Parrot's fave food:
seeds fruit grass leaves plant shoots

Big and small:
The tiny Pygmy parrot - less than 9cm (3.5") and 15g (0.5oz)

The Hyacinthine macaw – 1m (39") and 1.4kg (3 lbs)

"Eyes peeled for tree frogs!" said Mrs Parrot. "I've just seen one, Miss," cried Laxmi. "It was red with yellow spots!"

"I've just seen a monkey!" yelled Kelly.

"Cor, look at that flower!" said Charlotte. "It's got little ponds at the bottom of the leaves. And there are loads of tadpoles swimming about in them."

"That plant's a bromeliad," cried Mrs Parrot. "They attach themselves to the trunks and branches of fast-growing trees and hitch a lift up to the sun, taking their food and water from the air as they do. And those tadpoles are the young of poison-arrow frogs."

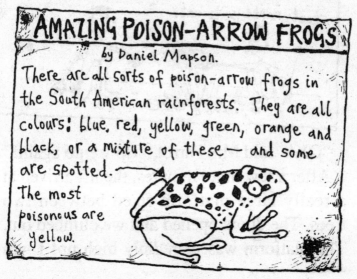

AMAZING POISON-ARROW FROGS
by Daniel Mapson.

There are all sorts of poison-arrow frogs in the South American rainforests. They are all colours: blue, red, yellow, green, orange and black, or a mixture of these — and some are spotted.

The most poisonous are yellow.

How they breed:

The mum frog lays the eggs in a burrow or in a bubble of jelly on a leaf.

The dad guards them.

When the tadpoles hatch the mum frog carries them on her back to the canopy.

She puts them in a puddle on a bromeliad plant (for safety).

How they got their name: Rainforest Indians hold poison—arrow frogs over fires which makes poisonous froth come out of their skin. They put this on their arrows which they use to shoot monkeys to eat.

"OK!" said Mrs Parrot, "Up we go again!"

After a few more minutes, the lift arrived at a really large platform fixed between two trees. The doors opened and we climbed out. The platform was incredibly high up! I was

50

really glad there were rails all the way around it. Joined on to the platform were walkways that led off into the nearby treetops where there were even more platforms and ladders. The whole place was completely ... AMAZING!

We went over to the rails and peered out into the mass of trees and leaves and at all the birds and insects that twittered and ticked and chirred in them. It felt like we were standing on the roof of a skyscraper!

"Ooer!" groaned Simon. "I've come over all dizzy!" Then he suddenly got down on his hands and knees and began crawling towards the centre of the platform.

"Hi!" said a woman carrying a large green backpack, who seemed to have come from nowhere.

"Yes, really, *really*, *really* high!" squeaked Simon. "Do you think you could help me down, please?"

"Relax!" said the woman, "You're quite safe on this platform. Welcome to the rainforest canopy, everyone! I'm Professor Palmtop. I'm here to show you around and answer your questions."

"I'd like to ask a question straight away then," I said. "Who put these walkways here? They're absolutely amazing!"

"They were built by the Brazilian government," said the professor. "They're about 50 metres above the ground – more or less at the top of the forest."

"Cripes!" said Kelly. "That's higher than my nan's block of flats and that's got 15 floors!"

"Oh no!" groaned Simon.

"Well, *you* may not like it up here," said Professor Palmtop, playfully ruffling Simon's hair, "but for us boffins, these platforms and the treetop walkways are a dream come true. The rainforest's canopy contains almost all of its wildlife and for years we've been really desperate to get up here and check it out. But we couldn't, so, until quite recently, it was all a complete mystery to us."

"Couldn't you just *climb* the trees?" said Laxmi.

"No way!" said the professor. "They're almost unclimbable, because there just aren't enough branches on the lower trunks. In the past, scientists have tried all sorts of ways of investigating life in the canopy. One of you might like to look them up some time. Some of the tricks the boffins dreamed up were really wacky!"

Scientists and the Rainforest Canopy

In the early days scientists nosed around the upper branches of fallen trees.

So, then they...

① Shot down branches with shotguns...

② Looked up mega-long telescopic poles...

③ Fired ropes into the trees to climb them...

④ Hired locals to climb trees...

⑤ Cut down whole trees...

⑥ Trained a monkey to collect plant samples...

⑦ Floated on a raft dangling from a hot air balloon...

Used construction cranes, ski lifts and ultra-light planes...

And then they built the walkways.

by Brian

"The walkways are actually quite a new idea," said the professor. "But they're definitely the most successful way to explore the canopy. They're great for scientists and really popular with tourists. Now, who's for a tree-top ramble?"

"Meeee!" everyone in the class yelled – except for Simon...

Lightning

So what do you think of our rainforest canopy?" asked Professor Palmtop as we all made our way along the walkway.

"It's er, really er ... *leafy*!" said Zoe, gazing around with her mouth open.

"It certainly is!" said Professor Palmtop. "If you look down at all these trees from an aeroplane it just looks like one unbroken green mass. The amazing thing is that, even though the branches of the various trees overlap, they hardly ever touch each other."

"Hey, I've just noticed something else!" said Brian. "The *leaves* don't touch either! And there must be billions of them!"

"That's right!" said the professor. "They don't! That allows each one to use every bit of its surface to convert sunlight to energy by photosynthesis.

"Oh, we know all about photosynthesis," said Kelly. "A Swiss cheese plant told us!"

"Oh, did it now?" said the professor, looking at Kelly as if she were a banana short of a bunch. "By the way," she added, "has anyone noticed anything about the shape of the leaves?"

"Yes, I have!" said Brian. "They're nearly all pointy."

"Right again!" said Professor Palmtop. "And those points are known as drip-tips. They're there to make sure rain runs off their surface. If the leaves stayed damp for any length of time moss  and fungus would start to grow on them."

"Why is it so noisy up here?" asked Zoe. "It's worse than Pickle Hill's dining room!"

"Good question!" said the professor. "Like all creatures, the animals of the canopy are very keen to protect their territory but – because of all the leaves – they can't actually see who's where and who rules which bit. So, generally speaking, everything up here hoots and hollers for all it's worth, just to let everything else know it's in its patch and that everything else should keep clear!"

We began making our way along the walkway and we hadn't gone far when Zoe said…

WHAT ARE THOSE BIG, BROWN DANGLY THINGS? THEY LOOK LIKE SOME SORT OF GIANT SEED POD.

Just as Zoe spoke one of the "seed pods" flew up above the treetops. Then all the others followed it!

"Those are fruit bats!" laughed the professor. "They sleep in the day and feed at night. I think we must have disturbed them. They're really useful to the rainforest because they eat fruit and drop masses of seeds, which grow into new bushes and trees."

"Cripes, they're massive!" said Brian.

Rainforest Bats by Zoe Thompson

Bats make up half of the mammals in the rainforest.

Smallest— ➤
Bumblebee bat from Thailand—the world's smallest mammal. Weighs less than a penny!

◄ **Biggest—**
Fruit bat with two metre wing-span

What bats eat:

Fruit

Flowers

Nectar

Blood ➤

Insects

Small Mammals ↓

Amazing fact: ➤ Some bats gobble up over 3,000 creepy crawlies every night. Yuk!

use sight to find food

Nectar eating bat ➤

feed in the dark

Long tongue like a humming bird

flowers bloom at night so it's easy for bats to find them!

59

"That," said Professor Palmtop, "is a sloth!"

"Yes, I am!" said the sloth. "So we'll have less of the big soft toy comments please."

"Mrs Parrot!" said Zoe, looking like her eyes might pop out of her head. "That sloth just spoke."

"Don't let it worry you, dear," said Mrs Parrot. "It's just a Pickle Hill sort of thing."

"Well, seeing as you've woken me," said the sloth. "We might as well get acquainted. You can call me Lightning. Ask me anything you want, just as long we don't have any comments about lazybones or layabouts!"

"Do you really er, *rest* for as long as people say you do?" said Laxmi.

"Well, I do sleep for 15 hours a day," said Lightning. "But I can't see what's wrong with that. I have to conserve my energy, you know."

"So what's your top speed then?" said Daniel.

"Oh, on a good day I can get up to about four mph," said Lightning.

"Four miles per hour!" said Daniel. "That seems quite good for a sloth."

"No," said Lightning. "Not four *miles* per hour! Four *metres* per hour! I like to take my time, you know."

"Excuse me, Lightning," said Charlotte. "But did you know there's slimy green stuff all over your fur?"

"Oh, you mean my *highlights*!" said Lightning. "Well, that's the little plant known as algae. It grows on my fur while I'm hanging from my tree here.  Comes in very useful as camouflage, especially when enemies are about! My fur's very interesting, you know. As you can see, it grows away from my chest so that I can drip-dry after it's rained. It's full of insects too, hundreds and hundreds of them! I'm a bugs' bed and breakfast!"

"It's true!" said Professor Palmtop. "One day, me and my scientist friends counted 950 different species of insect, all living in Lightning's fur!"

"Not bad, eh?" Lightning said proudly. "And we've even got our very own sloth moth. They can't live anywhere else but on us sloths. I'll show you one of mine if you like."

Lightning raised his arm and there, nestling in the fur of his armpit, was a moth.

HE'S MY CLOSEST FRIEND!

"The thing is," he continued, "about once every week, I have to climb down to the forest floor to go to the loo. Takes me yonks to get down there but, when I'm done, my sloth moths lay their eggs in my dung before snuggling down in my fur again. And once I'm finished I climb back up here. There'd be no point in me staying down there because I can't walk too well. That's because of these great big claws of mine. They're useless for walking but brilliant for hooking on to my tree here. They grip so powerfully that we even stay attached to our trees after we've died. But if you don't mind, I won't bother showing you that trick."

We all began to laugh but just then something huge, dark and dangerous-looking whizzed over the branches just above us and all the creatures in the trees around began screaming and screeching louder than ever.

"Cripes!" gasped Daniel. "What was *that*?"

"A harpy eagle, I think," said Professor Palmtop. "Lightning's number one enemy."

"Not half!" muttered Lightning. "Now, it was nice talking to you but would you mind moving off, so's not to draw attention to me. If that bird spots me, I'm sloth broth! Those harpy eagles are the biggest eagles in the whole world and us sloths are their favourite nosh!"

"Come on then, children," said Professor Palmtop. "Let's do as he asks. We can go up the last flight of steps to our highest viewing platform."

"This is what is known as the 'emergent' layer of the rainforest," said the professor when we reached the platform. "The treetops you can see poking out of the canopy belong to the oldest and tallest trees."

HEY LOOK, THERE'S THE HARPY EAGLE AGAIN!

OOER! I HOPE IT DOESN'T MISTAKE ONE OF US FOR A SLOTH!

EMERGENT LAYER: Macaws, Spider monkeys, Hummingbirds, Butterflies, Harpy eagles...

HARPY EAGLES by SIMON SIDWORTH

Giant harpy eagles are the kings of the rainforest treetops.

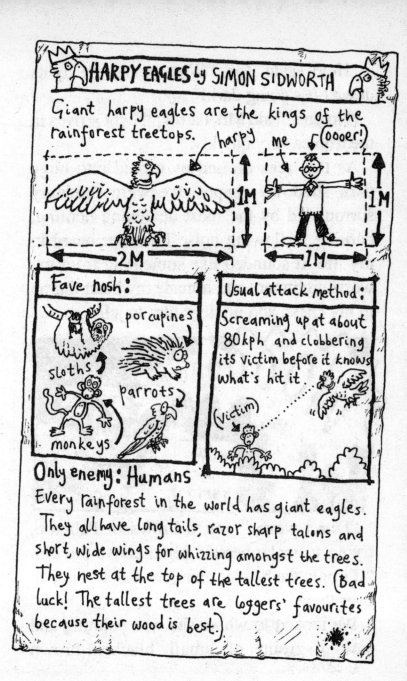

harpy

me (oooer!)

1M

1M

2M

1M

Fave nosh:

sloths

porcupines

monkeys

parrots

Usual attack method:

Screaming up at about 80kph and clobbering its victim before it knows what's hit it.

(Victim)

Only enemy: Humans

Every rainforest in the world has giant eagles. They all have long tails, razor sharp talons and short, wide wings for whizzing amongst the trees. They nest at the top of the tallest trees. (Bad luck! The tallest trees are loggers' favourites because their wood is best.)

"Hey!" said Zoe. "Who turned the lights down? It's going dark!"

"No one," said Mrs Parrot. "Night arrives in the tropics very quickly."

As the trees around us turned into huge dark shadowy shapes, we were suddenly surrounded by the most deafening hooting, barking, bellowing noise I've ever heard in my life. It sounded like something from my worst nightmare and it made my heart thump in my chest, and my legs turn to jelly.

"Don't worry," yelled Professor Palmtop, trying to make herself heard above the din. "It's only the howler monkeys. Look! They're over there."

We looked to where she was pointing and saw a group of small blackish-brown monkeys gathered in the branches about eight metres away from us.

"They do that to warn other animals to stay away from their territory," cried Mrs Parrot. "They probably think we're a rival group of monkeys."

"Speak for yourself," shouted Daniel.

"But it's so LOUD! I can hardly hear myself think!" yelled Brian. "I thought they'd be mega-massive!"

HOWLER MONKEYS
by Brian

Howler monkeys are about one metre tall, but are the loudest animal in the world. Even louder than lions!

WOOOOOOP!

ROAR! MIAOW!

Their howling can be heard up to five kilometres away! They've got a special voice box that makes their noise louder.

"I sometimes wish I had a voice as loud as a howler monkey," said Mrs Parrot. "It would come in really useful for playground duty and..."

All of a sudden Mrs Parrot peered at her watch.

"Oh, blimey!" she squawked. "That reminds me! I'm on playground duty in ten minutes. We'd better be getting back to Pickle Hill! Thanks for that, Professor Palmtop. It was most interesting!"

Then Mrs Parrot dashed back along the walkway, closely followed by the whole of class 5M. Ten minutes later we'd zoomed back down to Pickle Hill in the glass lift.

Grenville Globetrotter

The next day it was raining again, so Mrs Parrot decided we'd have our lunch break indoors and watch a video while we ate our snacks. We went to get our lunch boxes from the cloakroom but we'd only been in there for two seconds when Simon shouted, "Hey! Someone's pinched my chocolate bar!"

Suddenly, it seemed as if everyone was discovering that their snacks had vanished.

We all rushed out of the cloakroom and told Mrs Parrot about the missing snacks but she didn't seem in the slightest bit bothered. She just smiled sweetly and pointed at our telly. Grinning out at us from the screen was an elegant, bearded, red-faced man wearing old-fashioned clothes and a big ruff. He was sitting on a wooden barrel on the deck of an ancient sailing ship. But more to the point, he was holding Daniel's fizzy drink and  the rest of our missing snacks!

"Heh heh!" he laughed. "Got yer going there, didn't I?" Then he began to take the wrapper off Simon's chocolate bar.

"Miss!" yelled Simon, looking like he'd burst into tears at any moment. "That man's going to eat my chocolate!"

"No, I'm not," said the man. "I just wanted to show you that, without the rainforests, you wouldn't have a single one of these yummy goodies! You should all be very grateful to the tropical jungles!" Then his hand popped out of the TV screen and he gave Simon his chocolate back!

"Er, thanks," said Simon, looking completely gobsmacked. "Thanks very much, Mr ... er..."

"Globetrotter's the name," said the man. "Sir Grenville Globetrotter, sea captain, explorer and businessman. About five hundred years ago me an' a whole host of other brave seafaring coves began roaming the world's oceans in search of riches and adventure. Many of our travels led us to tropical jungles where we found a different sort of treasure from the gold that we'd hoped for. In other words, we found the tasty treasures  that grow in the rainforest! For instance, take that there choccy bar. Now, where do you think that came from?"

"Safebury's!" shouted Kelly.

"No, I mean in the first place!" barked Sir Grenville.

"Not the foggiest," said Kelly.

"It comes from these!" said Grenville, and he held out a handful of brown seedpods. "These are the seeds of the rainforest cocoa tree. The Aztec and Mayan Indians used to  grind them up and mix them with water and hot chillis to make a drink they later named chocoatl."

"It means foam water!" cried Mrs Parrot. "That's where we get our word *chocolate* from!"

"Christopher Columbus brought cocoa beans back to Europe," said Sir Grenville. "Years later, someone had the bright idea of mixing the cocoa drink with sugar."

"Sugar also came from the rainforest," added Mrs Parrot. "After that, drinking and eating chocolate really caught on!"

"But Sir Grenville," said Zoe. "Why did you take my banana?"

"They're from the rainforest too," said Sir Grenville. "The Arabs first brought them back from the Asian jungles. Their name comes from an Arabic word meaning finger."

"Now bananas are grown in tropical places all over the world!" said Mrs Parrot. "But when they were first brought to Britain, people had no idea what to do with them. Some people even ate bananas with their skins on!"

"But what about my cola drink?" said Daniel.

"From the jungle too," said Sir Grenville. "In 1880, a doctor in America invented a drink using crushed seeds from the cola tree and the leaves of the coca bush. He meant it to be used as medicine, but it became so popular that people began drinking it for refreshment."

"And now," said Mrs Parrot, "more than 800 *million* cola drinks are slurped down around the world every single day! But nowadays the taste comes from artificial flavours rather than from cola plants and coca bushes."

"And my chewing gum?" asked Brian.

"Also from the rainforest," said Sir Grenville.

CHEWING GUM by Brian

Rainforest Indians cut the bark of sapodilla trees. This made milky, rubbery stuff called chicle dribble out. They chewed the chicle to clean their teeth and refresh their mouths — and maybe to look cool?

SWOON!

In the 1880s an American mixed chicle with sugar and flavouring to make chewing gum to sell. American people soon went crazy for it.

Yeeee-ha!

"And this first came from the rainforest too!" said Sir Grenville. He reached out of the screen, picked up Mrs Parrot's mug of coffee from right under her nose and took a big slurp.

VERY REFRESHING! THANK YOU!

"But you still haven't told us what *you* were bringing back from the rainforests," I said.

"Nutmegs from south-east Asia!" said Sir Grenville. "You could buy a sack of them for a penny in the East Indies then sell it in London for hundreds of pounds!"

"And I suppose you're going to tell us that the pineapples for Charlotte's drink and the sweetcorn for Laxmi's corn chips first came from the rainforest," I said.

"Of course!" said Sir Grenville.

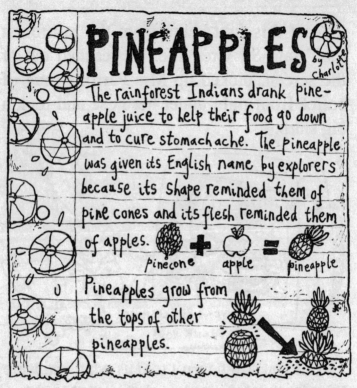

PINEAPPLES
by Charlotte

The rainforest Indians drank pine-apple juice to help their food go down and to cure stomach ache. The pineapple was given its English name by explorers because its shape reminded them of pine cones and its flesh reminded them of apples.

pinecone **+** apple **=** pineapple

Pineapples grow from the tops of other pineapples.

"But that's not all!" continued Sir Grenville. "Come and see this lot!"

The next moment the picture on the screen changed and we all gasped. Sir Grenville was now standing outside a supermarket holding on to an enormous shopping trolley! He waved to us, then pushed his trolley into the shop and began grabbing things off the shelves. Soon, other shoppers noticed him and in no time a little crowd was following him.

When his trolley was full to overflowing, Sir Grenville stopped and said, "And there's plenty more where this lot came from. There are still more than 2,500 different sorts of fruit growing in the rainforest that people from the western world haven't even tasted yet!

"I think we'll leave Sir Grenville to sort out his purchases," said Mrs Parrot. "It's time we took a closer look at the rainforest floor. But first I'll need some help to roll back our classroom lino!"

"Why?" said Charlotte.

"You'll see in a minute!" said Mrs Parrot, with a grin.

Getting down to earth

As we began rolling back the lino Mrs Parrot said, "There are tonnes of interesting plants and animals down on the rainforest floor – like fabulous fungi, amazing anteaters and giant anaconda snakes!"

AND ADDERS TOO?

NO WAY, KELLY! THEY'RE ALL IN THE MATHS CORNER!

"And there are masses of bugs too," Mrs Parrot continued. "The rainforest's absolutely teeming with all sorts of amazing creepy crawlies! Millions of species haven't even been discovered yet. An acre of rainforest can contain as many as 12,000 different sorts of beetle. And one single rainforest tree in Peru was found to have 43 types of ant in it!"

Soon the lino was moved out of the way. But, instead of a hard classroom floor underneath, there was spongy, smelly, damp earth covered with leaves and sticks.

"Yikes!" gasped Simon. "We're on the rainforest floor!"

"And more to the point," squeaked Zoe, "we've shrunk. We're the size of raisins!"

She was right! Absolutely everything around us now looked mega-massive, times about a hundred! Twigs looked like telegraph poles and small crumbs of soil appeared to be the size of huge boulders. We were at the side of a rainforest path, which seemed as wide as a ten-lane motorway! It was extremely busy too, with all sorts of extremely weird insect traffic and quite a few odd-looking mammals hopping and scurrying along it. And they were all travelling in the same direction!

"Hey!" said Zoe. "This is ace. We've got the bug's-eye view. I used to get down on the ground with mini-beasts like this when I was small." Then she pointed to the creepy crawlies that were rushing past and said, "But what's the matter with that lot? They all look like they're running away from something!"

"They are! They are!" cried Mrs Parrot.

 Suddenly, a little pile of leaves and twigs that had been lying at the side of the track got up and ran away.

"Wow! Whatever's coming must be really scary!" said Daniel. "Did you see that? Even the leaves are running away!"

"They were insects," said Mrs Parrot. "They're just camouflaged to *look* like leaves."

Just then, we all heard a terrible hissing sound and smelled a horrible smell. Something quite big and awful must be coming along the forest path…

"Right on time!" added Mrs Parrot, with a

satisfied smile. "Now children, keep calm. And enjoy the show!"

At that moment the most horrendous thing I've ever seen in my whole life came around the corner. At first I thought it was some sort of prehistoric monster but then I realized what it was!

It was a HUGE ant. And it was followed by another one. Then another. Soon, hundreds and hundreds of the massive things were charging past us. Their footsteps sounding like thunder while they made the horrid hissing we'd heard and gave off that awful smell.

"Wh… what are they?" stammered Brian.

"Army ants," said Mrs Parrot. "Some of the most fearsome insects in the South American rainforest. But we're in no danger. We're sort of invisible."

Even though she said this, it was still pretty terrifying to see those huge creatures go charging past. They must have been about 12 millimetres long, but at our present size they looked as big as buffalo! And there were thousands of them!

Three of the ants suddenly seized a large spider and ripped it to shreds while several others set about a terrified, tiny mouse-like creature and turned it into a skeleton in what seemed like seconds.

"It looks horrible but they're only doing what comes naturally," said Mrs Parrot.

"Do the army ants ever eat people, Mrs Parrot?" whispered Zoe.

"Not normally," said Mrs Parrot. "Most humans and large animals get out of the way pretty quickly. However, army ants have attacked and eaten farm animals that have been left tied up. It's said they can polish off a whole horse in a few hours!"

"What happens if there's a village in their path?" said Simon.

"Well, rainforest Indians use them as pest controllers. They move out of their houses for a couple of days, taking their food with them, and leave the army ants to chew up all the cockroaches, mice, fleas and other vermin."

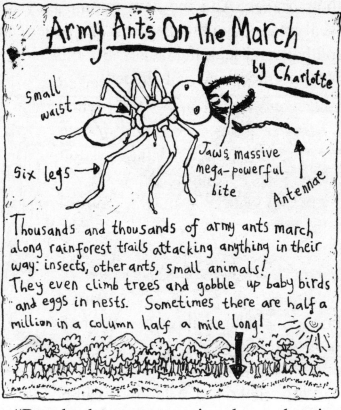

"But do the army ants just keep charging around the rainforest trashing everything in their path?" said Harry. "Don't they *ever* stop?"

"Well, as you'll see any moment now, they're not always this ... er ... *'anti*-social'!" said Mrs Parrot, with a giggle. "And yes, they do stop."

As she spoke, the ants all seemed to put on their brakes. And the next minute they all went into a huge huddle, a bit like American footballers discussing tactics. But this huddle was enormous and ball-shaped!

"Flip!" said Zoe. "Whatever are they doing?"

"That's a mystery you can solve, Zoe," said Mrs Parrot. "I'll let you investigate it for your homework."

The Mystery of the Ant Ball

Solved by Zoe!!

1 Medium-size worker army ants carry larvae (the little grubs that turn into baby ants). These larvae give off pheromones (squirts of chemical) which make all the army ants keep on rampaging.

SMELL

Ooooh! Rampage!

2 When the larvae are almost ready to become pupae (the last stage of their development before they finally become ants) the pheromone-squirting stops.

No SMELL

Ooer! Don't know what came over me!

3 The army ants stop charging and go into a ball. It's got corridors and rooms which are where the pupae are stored. The whole thing is known as a bivouac and is made from nothing but thousands of ants clinging to each other!

(It's like a block of flats made entirely from humans!)

I'm sure these walls have ears...

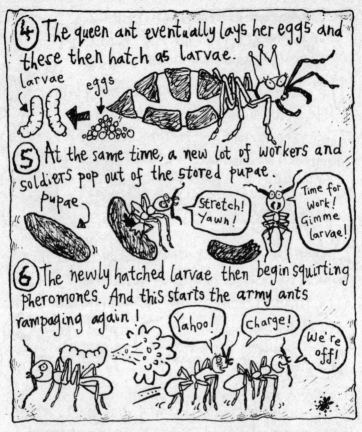

"While the ants are busy huddling we'll have a proper look at the forest floor," said Mrs Parrot, and we began examining all the smelly, damp stuff that lay scattered around us.

"Some of the soil's not all that fertile," said Mrs Parrot. "So the trees' roots don't go very deep. Instead trees put out these big above-ground support roots called buttress roots."

"As dead leaves and wood falls to the floor, it gets turned into compost by the heat, damp, bacteria and the millions of insects that live down here. This is what feeds the trees."

"What are these?" said Kelly, pointing to some little green leaves poking out of the ground.

"A tree seedling," said Mrs Parrot. "In a hundred years that might well be a 30-metre-tall kapok tree! Or a giant mahogany! The seeds that the seedlings grow from are mostly spread by wind, birds and animals."

"Look, Mrs Parrot!" cried Daniel. "I've found a seed! I've found a seed!" He was staggering towards us carrying a seed that looked at least twice as big as a rugby ball.

"Oh yes, Daniel," said Mrs Parrot. "That's a rumberry seed. Rumberries are wonderfully tasty little tropical fruits – and that seed is really tiny! It looks like a monkey ate the rumberries and the seeds dropped out in its poo."

The smile suddenly disappeared from Daniel's face. He dropped the seed and quickly began wiping his hands on his trousers.

Suddenly, Kelly screamed and pointed. We all turned to see a massive brown creature making its way towards us through the heaps of leaves and twigs. It looked as big as two elephants and it was making an awful hissing noise! Just like the army ants ... but even louder!

"What is it?" yelled Charlotte. "What *is* it?"

"Oh dear!" gasped Mrs Parrot, suddenly looking really worried. "It's a Goliath tarantula! A giant, bird-eating spider! Quick! Follow me, let's get out of the way!"

Mrs Parrot dashed behind a heap of rotting leaves and we all followed.

There was a flash of green quite near the spider and a tiny lizard suddenly shot out of the leaves. The spider was on it in a second and sank its huge fangs into the lizard's neck.

"Just think, Kelly," said Daniel, as we watched the spider drag the lizard off. "That could have been *you*!"

"If it had got you, all that would be left of you would be skin, bones and hair!" said Mrs Parrot.

"What's the matter, Kelly?" said Daniel. "You look a bit pale."

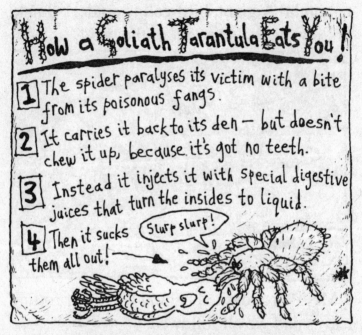

How a Goliath Tarantula Eats You!

1. The spider paralyses its victim with a bite from its poisonous fangs.

2. It carries it back to its den — but doesn't chew it up, because it's got no teeth.

3. Instead it injects it with special digestive juices that turn the insides to liquid.

4. Then it sucks them all out!

Slurp slurp!

"Some rainforest Indians roast tarantulas over their campfires, and eat them," said Mrs Parrot.

"Yuk!" said the whole class.

"Now, I really do think we've had enough scary moments for the time being," said Mrs Parrot. "It's time we grew up and got back to Pickle Hill!"

She glanced about and then said, "Where's Laxmi?"

We all looked around. There was no sign of Laxmi anywhere!

"I haven't seen her for yonks," said Simon.

"Maybe the army ants got her!" cried Charlotte.

"Don't panic!" said Mrs Parrot. "We'll try calling for her."

We all shouted Laxmi's name as loud as we could and a moment later we heard a muffled but echoey sort of reply. It was coming from a big, greeny-yellow plant, shaped a bit like an ice-cream cone.

"Oh no!" yelled Mrs Parrot.

"What's the matter?" gasped Zoe.

"That's a carnivorous pitcher plant!" cried Mrs Parrot. "Laxmi must have fallen into it. It's a meat-eater! They also squirt out yucky juices that digest their prey. If we don't get Laxmi out quickly she'll be schoolgirl soup!"

We all crawled up a small log next to the pitcher plant then peered down into it. There at the bottom of the plant, looking extremely scared, was Laxmi Sharma.

"I climbed up on to the log to get away from the giant spider!" she yelled. "But then I slipped and fell into this. I've been trying to climb out for ages!"

She began to scramble up the sloping inside surface of the plant, but it was covered with downward-pointing hairy things. Every time she reached one she couldn't get past it and just slid back down to the bottom again.

HELP ME!
HELP ME!

"That's exactly how they trap the flies and lizards that fall into them!" Mrs Parrot said calmly. "But don't worry Laxmi. We'll soon think of a way to get you out of there."

"We could try lowering down a rope," suggested Kelly.

"*What* rope, Kelly?" said Daniel. "We haven't got one!"

"Well, we could find a stick or something for her to climb up, then," said Kelly.

At that moment we heard a crack of thunder and felt some large wet blobs hit us. They were raindrops! But, at our present size, they felt more like rain *clouds*! More and more hit us. Soon, it was like someone was emptying hundreds of baths of water over us!

HURRAH! IT'S THE AFTERNOON DOWNPOUR!

Mrs Parrot peered down at Laxmi and yelled, "Laxmi, as the plant fills with water, start swimming! When you get to the top, we'll pull you out!"

While the deafening thunder rolled around us, the rain chucked down and the pitcher plant slowly filled with water. Laxmi doggy-paddled like crazy and eventually rose to the lip.

"Thank goodness for that!" gasped Mrs Parrot, as we finally hauled Laxmi out.

But the pitcher plant wasn't the only thing that was filling up with water! The forest floor was now beginning to flood and, what with us being so small, we were soon up to our waists in swirling mud!  Just when it seemed like we'd have to swim for our lives, the flood seemed to drain away. And, after a minute or two, it was only up to our ankles!

"Cripes!" said Kelly. "Where did the water go?"

"Nowhere," said Daniel. "We've grown. Look!"

He pointed at our feet and we saw that we were now standing in a big muddy puddle. On our own classroom floor!

"Hurrah!" cried Brian. "We're back at Pickle Hill."

Makangy and Emaka

"Mrs Parrot," said Zoe. "Do many people live in the rainforests?"

"Yes, dear," said Mrs Parrot. "But not nearly as many as there used to be. For instance, in the Amazon in the nineteenth century there were at least six million rainforest Indians. But now there are only 200,000. Often they've had their land taken by settlers or big businesses, and many died from diseases they've caught from people arriving from the big cities."

"And are there really people living in the rainforests who haven't been discovered by modern people?" said Simon.

"Yes, some people do still live deep in the forests without any modern gadgets at all," said Mrs Parrot. "No electricity, no phones, no piped water, not even any wheels!"

"Wow!" said Brian. "Like prehistoric people!"

"Exactly!" said Mrs Parrot. "One of the groups we do know about are the South American Yanomami. They were discovered about 30 years ago by pilots flying over the Amazon rainforest. Not long afterwards, people from the cities went into the jungle and made contact with them. It was like the Yanomami had been living in the Stone Age one week and modern times the next. Tragically, many of them died of modern diseases that hadn't existed in their group before."

"Do they all have a modern lifestyle now?" said Charlotte.

"No," said Mrs Parrot. "Many try to stick to their traditional ways. They live in big round houses called yanos, don't read or write, and don't have names for the days of the week or the months of the year."

"So are all the rainforest people just in the Amazon?" said Kelly.

"No," said Mrs Parrot. "There are millions more living in rainforests all around the world, much as they've done for thousands of years. We'll go and visit some if you like!"

"How?" said Kelly.

"Easy-peasy!" chuckled Mrs Parrot. She pointed to a little trapdoor in our classroom ceiling (which none of us could ever remember seeing before). As she spoke, the trapdoor opened and a long creeper slid down from it.

Mrs Parrot shinned up it, quicker than a monkey, and cried, "What are you all waiting for then? Up you come!"

I was the first to climb up. It was quite easy, just like the climbing ropes in PE. But I am a brilliant gymnast (and not at all big-headed). Simon slid back down the creeper (about a billion times!), but in the end we all got up there, and Mrs Parrot helped us scramble through the hatch. But instead of being in a dusty attic we were back on a warm, damp forest floor (full-sized this time, phew!), surrounded by huge gnarled trees, twisting green creepers, chattering monkeys, scurrying lizards, and buzzing insects. Plus lots and lots of wet, clammy heat!

"Jeepers Creepers!" cried Daniel. "Where are we now, Mrs Parrot?"

"Africa, dear!" cried Mrs Parrot. "This is the central African country known as Cameroon. Nearly all of Africa's rainforests are in the middle of the continent."

"Look!" said Kelly. "There's a boy over there."

We looked to where she pointed and saw a boy walking towards us. From his size I guessed that he was about the same age as us. He wasn't wearing any clothes, apart from

some brown stuff around his middle. He was carrying a small axe and had a length of forest creeper looped round his waist. Attached to it were lots of folded leaves, which looked like shopping bags.

"That's not a boy," said Mrs Parrot. "It's a man. He's a pygmy! The pygmies are groups of African rainforest dwellers who never grow more than a metre and a half tall because they've adapted to life in the rainforest over thousands of years. Their smallness lets them move about easily in the dense undergrowth while their light weight makes it a doddle for them to shin up trees!"

The little man had now reached us. He smiled and said, "Hello everyone. My name is Makangy, I am pleased to meet you. Welcome to the rainforest. I belong to the Baka people and this is where I live with my family and the others in our group. Come and see my home."

Makangy led us all to a clearing in the forest where there were about ten green huts made from sticks covered with leaves. A woman and two really small children came out of one of them.

"This is Emaka, my wife," said Makangy. "And these are my children, Dondola and Mogemba." We smiled at the children and they grinned and waved at us shyly.

"I like your house!" said Daniel. "It reminds me of a den I once made in my garden."

"Thank you," said Makangy. "We like it too. But soon we must move on to other parts of the forest where there is more food."

"And then will someone else come and live in your house?" said Zoe.

"Yes, the snakes and birds and ants!" laughed Emaka. "And it will fall down and go back to nature. But that is not a problem. Our group moves often. Me and the other women soon make new places wherever we go."

"And do you stay in the forest all the time?" said Laxmi.

"Yes," said Makangy. "We get all we need to live from the forest. See, even my little middle covering is made from the bark of the tree."

I SUPPOSE YOU HAVE TO KEEP WELL AWAY FROM YOUR CAMP FIRE WEARING THAT!

YES I DO. HA HA HA! YOU ARE A VERY FUNNY BOY!

"But what do you do for food?" said Charlotte. "Don't you have shops?"

Makangy looked puzzled for a moment then shook his head and said, "I have never eaten one of these shop things. Are they tasty?"

"We get lots of good things from the forest," said Emaka. "I go out every day with the other women and collect mushrooms, roots, nuts, nice fat beetle grubs, plants and juicy caterpillars for us to eat. And while we are doing that, Makangy and the men get the bush meat!"

"I didn't even know meat *grew* on bushes!" said Daniel.

"It doesn't, Daniel," said Mrs Parrot. "The forest is sometimes called 'the Bush'. Bush meat is Makangy's name for the wild animals that he and his group hunt for food."

"That is right!" said Makangy. "We use our dogs and nets and our bows and arrows to trap and kill wild creatures – animals like antelope, birds, wild cats and monkeys."

"Monkeys!" said Zoe, in a shocked voice.

"Oh yes," said Makangy. "They're very tasty! And elephants too. Sometimes I go out on my own and kill elephants with my spear, but sometimes I do it with my friends."

"We also get food from the forest streams," said Emaka. "I do that by making a ... a ... *block* in them!"

"A dam!" I said.

"That is it!" said Emaka. "We make a dam. Come, I will show you!"

We followed her to a place where she'd blocked a stream with stones and sticks and mud. A bit further down from the dam the stream bed was almost empty, with lots of little fish and shrimps flipping around in the shallow water.

COME... YOU CAN HELP US CATCH THEM!

We helped scoop the fish into Emaka's basket, "Now we will make the water come back so the other fish will still have a home," she said. "Wherever we take our food from we are careful never to take too much because we want all the wild things to be here for ever."

We helped Emaka break down the dam so that water rushed back along the stream bed.

"Sometimes we make a trade to get different things," she said. "We take bush meat and medicine plants to the farming people who live near the edge of the forest and they give us knives, cloth, cooking pots and bananas for eating."

Then Makangy sighed and said, "But our most favourite thing to eat is the honey of forest bees. I use the honey-guide to find where the bees' nests are."

"So, what is this honey-guide?" said Zoe. "Some sort of book?"

Makangy looked puzzled again and said, "I do not know what a book is but the honey-guide is a bird. See, there is one now."

He pointed to a branch a few metres away where a little bird was hopping around and calling over and over again.

"Good! Good!" said Makangy excitedly. "It wants to take us to a bees' nest right now. Follow and you will see!"

And with that he dashed off into the forest.

We all ran after Makangy and the honey-guide. They went really fast but every now and again the bird would land on a branch and call until we caught up with it, then fly off again.

After we'd dashed along the forest trail for a few minutes it finally landed in a really tall tree. High up, in the space between the trunk and a branch, was a bees' nest. Makangy now did something amazing. If we hadn't seen it with our own eyes we wouldn't have believed it was possible!

MAKANGY CUT NOTCHES IN THE TREE TRUNK WITH HIS AXE.

HE STRAPPED HIMSELF TO THE TREE TRUNK WITH A CREEPER AROUND HIS WAIST. HE PUT HIS FEET IN THE NOTCHES AND PULLED HIMSELF UP.

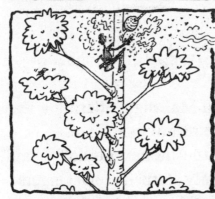

WHEN MAKANGY REACHED THE BEES' NEST HE SMOKED THEM OUT.

MAKANGY CLIMBED DOWN WITH THE HONEY IN THE FOLDED LEAVES HANGING ON HIS BELT.

Makangy climbed back down to the ground. "That was like Jack going up the beanstalk," laughed Daniel, "to find the bees that lay the golden honey!"

Makangy opened up one of the bundles and offered some to Kelly. She stuck her fingers in, then licked them.

HEY! IT'S BRILLIANT!

"Try some!" said Makangy, offering a leaf full of honey to the rest of us.

"But where's the honey-guide?" said Laxmi, as we happily slurped at our fingers.

"Getting its reward for leading Makangy to the nest," said Mrs Parrot. "See! It's helping itself to leftover grubs and honeycomb."

As we watched the honey-guide flitting in and out of the bees' nest, Emaka began making a small fire.

"Now we will have our favourite part!" she said, taking a large chunk of waxy honeycomb and holding it over the fire. We immediately saw that not only was the honeycomb full of honey, it also had grubs and larvae and even a few bees in it! As the honey softened with the heat the grubs began to squirm. Then, when it was really squishy and drippy, Makangy and his family scooped it out and put it in their mouths ... grubs and bees and all!

"The best!" spluttered Makangy, through a honey mouthful. "The wriggly grubs make it slide down more nicely!"

"Yuk!" said Zoe, but very quietly so they wouldn't hear.

"Now!" said Emaka. "We will celebrate our honey find with music!" And then she ran into the stream with Dondola and Mogemba.

When the water was up to their waists, Emaka and the children suddenly raised their hands and, with their palms cupped, they began beating on the surface. It made a brilliant drumming noise! Each one of them tapped out their own pattern of beats and all the different rhythms made a really exciting sound.

"So why don't you all try some water-drumming?" said Makangy.

"Why not!" cried Mrs Parrot, before leaping into the stream and beating the water! A moment later we all joined her and began doing our own water-drumming. We weren't as good as the Baka people, but Daniel (who's got his own drum kit at home) did some very fancy slapping and splashing.

Brian suddenly looked up at the tree tops and said, "Er, Mrs Parrot, do the bees get really annoyed about having their nests robbed."

"Yes, they do," said Mrs Parrot. "When they've recovered from the effects of the smoke they sometimes even chase the honey gatherers back to their camp. Why?"

"Because a huge swarm of them is heading this way!" said Brian.

He was right. Zooming towards us was a very large cloud of very angry bees.

"I think it's time we buzzed off!" said Mrs Parrot.

And with that we all scrambled out of the stream and quickly squeezed through a gap in the trees. Then we found ourselves back in our classroom!

Phew! What a relief that was. I must say, when it comes to getting us out of tight spots, Mrs Parrot really is the *bee's knees*!

Eric the Eco-warrior

Straight after break time we began sketching and making notes about the amazing things we'd seen in the Cameroon rainforest. Kelly tried to draw a picture of Makangy climbing the tree but after making two or three strokes with her pencil she decided it wasn't any good, screwed it into a ball and was just about to throw it into the waste paper bin when a thin man with red spiky hair popped out of our paper cupboard. He was wearing bright green overalls and was covered from head to toe with masses of badges and stickers.

"Don't do that!" he yelled, looking straight at Kelly. "Have you tried rubbing it out! Or using both sides! Don't you realize what a precious resource that paper is!"

"It doesn't grow on trees you know," Daniel whispered with a snigger.

"Oh yes it does! And thanks to me and my pals, the big paper-makers are at last making an effort to use wood from fast-growing trees so that many of the world's forests will be spared!" yelled the spiky-haired man. "But that doesn't mean that everything's OK in the rainforests! No way!"

And then he turned to Mrs Parrot and said, "Sorry I'm late, Mrs P. I had a bit of a bust-up with a chap who threw a crisp packet out of his car window. Moron!"

"That's all right," said Mrs Parrot with a smile. She turned to us and said, "Children, I'd like you to meet Eric Woodbine. He's an environmental activist."

"Eco-warrior, *actually*!" said Eric, with a grin, "And I'm here to tell you how rainforests all over the world are being destroyed. Now, I want you all to count out loud to sixty!"

We did as we were told and when we'd finished Eric said, "While you were counting, it's estimated that somewhere in the world, 100 acres of rainforest was destroyed. That's an area as big as 60 football pitches. So in 24 hours an area of rainforest the size of *86,400* soccer pitches would be destroyed!"

SO WHERE ARE THEY GOING TO HOLD ALL THE FOOTBALL MATCHES THEN?

HE DOESN'T MEAN REAL FOOTBALL PITCHES. HE'S JUST TRYING TO SHOW US WHAT A HUGE AMOUNT OF RAINFOREST IS DESTROYED EACH DAY.

"That's right!" said Eric. "And it'll happen again tomorrow. And the day after that. Experts have estimated that the world is losing 137 plant, animal and insect species every single day due to rainforest destruction. That's 50,000 species a year. But it won't just be plants and animals that the world will be losing!"

"We'll be losing the trees that recycle the polluting carbon stuff," said Laxmi. "Trees that give the world oxygen!"

"Exactly!" said Eric. "And then there's all the amazing medicine we get from the rainforests. Twenty per cent of all the drugs we use contain extracts from rainforest plants. For example, the rosy periwinkle from Madagascar gives us a drug that prevents cancer.

"And we haven't even begun to make the most of the medicines from the rainforest. So far, less than one per cent of tropical trees and plants have been tested by scientists for helpful drugs they might contain. There's no telling what life-saving ingredients they might find! But the thing is, at the rate the rainforest's being destroyed, the plants will be gone before scientists can discover them!"

"So why don't governments just stop the rainforests being destroyed?" said Laxmi.

"It's not that simple," said Eric. "Sometimes it's the governments themselves who destroy the forests. Other times it's big businesses. And sometimes it's the poor people who live in and around them. They're often so desperate for money, food and somewhere to live that they don't realize what terrible damage they're doing to their own environment. For instance, the poor people from the shanty towns of Rio de Janeiro in Brazil go into the local rainforest park and kill the animals because they've nothing else to eat. But enough facts, it's time you saw for yourselves…"

Two minutes later we were all standing around our wildlife garden and pond.

"It's a rainforest!" said Eric. Then he took a bottle of Garden-Gro (Extra-Strength Jungle-Juice Formula) out of his pocket, gave our garden a swift squirt and waved his hand over it a couple of times. Suddenly, where the wildflowers had been just seconds earlier there were now little rainforest trees, tiny screeching monkeys, even tinier squawking parrots ... the whole blooming lot!

But the rainforest and its creatures didn't stay little for long. As we stood and watched in disbelief the whole lot began to grow up around us really fast. Soon, we were completely surrounded by giant trees, saplings, creepers and noisy animals.

Just then we saw something large, orange and hairy in the trees above Eric and we gasped.

"What's *that*?" cried Daniel.

"That," said Eric, "is a female orang-utan. A magnificent specimen too."

"Cor look at it go!" said Laxmi, as it began to swing from branch to branch. "It's so … er …"

"Gymnastic!" cried Brian.

"Exactly!" said Eric. "They swing from branch to branch using their very long and powerful arms and those hook-shaped hands and feet."

"Ah, look!" said Kelly. "There's a baby one. It wants to follow the mum to the tree but it can't get across."

"Yes, but look what's happening now!" said Charlotte.

SEE, ITS MUM HAS MADE IT A LIVING BRIDGE.

"Brilliant, aren't they?" said Eric, as the orang-utans swung back up into the canopy. Then he looked sad and said, "There used to be orang-utans all over south-east Asia but thanks to the logging companies destroying their habitat the only places they live now are here on Borneo and on the island of Sumatra. Now, follow me kids!"

We all followed Eric and, after we'd walked a few hundred metres along the trail, Brian said, "Can anyone hear that noise?"

"Yes," said Laxmi. "I can. It's like machines or something."

I could hear it now. It was a sort of roaring, growling noise and as we walked on it got louder by the minute.

"It's the loggers!" whispered Eric.

We ducked down and crept after Eric. We could now smell burning and hear voices as well as loud machine noises. Suddenly, through a gap in the trees we saw them! A huge muddy clearing had been made in the forest. It was surrounded by massive piles of logs and there seemed to be men and machines everywhere. Two enormous yellow bulldozers with a chain stretched between them were charging through the forest knocking down smaller trees. A bit closer to us, two men were operating a huge red chainsaw which screamed as its teeth bit into the trunk of a giant tree.

"It's like the end of the world!" gasped Zoe.

"You're not far wrong!" said Eric. "That tree's taken at least a hundred years to grow. And those men will destroy it in minutes! That's what I'm trying to stop!"

The saw cut through the last part of the tree trunk. The loggers jumped out of the way and the tree crashed down. Suddenly we heard screams and howls and screeches. Animals were coming out of the fallen tree and rushing off into the jungle.

"It's the creatures that were too frightened to come down when the sawing started!" said Eric. "They don't stand much of a chance of finding a new home. What's left of the forest round here will probably be burned."

"This logging company bought thousands of acres of Borneo rainforest from local tribespeople," said Eric bitterly. "The rainforest had been their home for centuries but the money the logging company paid them for it was so little that it was only enough to buy two cans of cola for each tribe member. Since then the loggers have destroyed about a third of the Borneo rainforest and thrown the rainforest people off the land. And now they make the locals work for them for next to nothing!"

We watched in stunned silence. Then Eric turned sadly and said, "Let's go. I've got one more thing to show you."

We followed Eric and, after walking for a few more minutes, he signalled us to stop.

"The forests are full of good stuff that people want," he said. "Like wood for making furniture and buildings. The problem is, the logging companies usually want it all and want it straight away. This means that once it's taken, the forest is gone for ever! But it doesn't have to be like that."

He pointed to some really smooth tree trunks that were growing by the path, then he said, "Does anyone know what these are?"

"But I thought bamboo was thin stuff!" said Kelly. "Grandad grows his runner beans up bamboo canes. This stuff is ginormous, thicker than me!"

"I'd never realized bamboo trees could grow so big!" said Brian.

"Bamboo's not a tree," said Eric. "It's a type of grass!"

"Well, I wouldn't want to mow this lawn!" joked Daniel.

"People do cut lots and lots of bamboo," laughed Eric. "Millions of them depend on it for their livelihood. Believe it or not, over a billion of the world's people live in bamboo houses."

"But doesn't that mean all the bamboo will get used up, just like the trees?" said Laxmi.

"No," said Eric "That's the brilliant thing about bamboo. It's incredibly fast-growing. Some sorts can grow up to a metre in a single day! A 20-metre tree cut down by the loggers takes 60 *years* to grow again. A 20-metre bamboo takes only 60 *days* to grow again!"

"So it's what they call a renewable resource!" said Mrs Parrot. "Properly looked after it will provide goodies for hundreds of years to come. And there's no reason why the rest of the rainforest trees can't be looked after in a similar way! If only people weren't so greedy."

"Exactly!" said Eric. "Some people call bamboo the gold of the east. It's used for so many different things that scientists believe that long ago there may have been a Bamboo Age, just like there was a Stone Age and an Iron Age. There are at least a thousand different sorts of bamboo and it's got more than 1,500 uses. Here I'll show you some!"

Eric led us through a gap in the bamboo and we were suddenly in a huge clearing.

"Cripes!" said Zoe. "Everything's made from bamboo!"

"I don't know about you lot," laughed Daniel, "but I feel completely ... *bamboo*zled!"

"It's time for us to go inside the bamboo house" said Mrs Parrot.

We followed her up the steps into the house. And the moment we entered it, it seemed very, very familiar.

"Hey!" said Kelly. "This room's got bamboo blinds across the windows. Just like the ones in our classr–"

"Er, Mrs Parrot," said Laxmi. "This *is* our classroom, isn't it! Does this mean we're back at..."

"Pickle Hill!" cried Mrs Parrot excitedly. "Yes, we are! And that's more or less the end of our rainforest lesson. I hoped you've all enjoyed it."

"It was brill!" said Daniel.

"Absolutely ace!" the rest of us agreed.

"Thank you! Thank you!" said Mrs Parrot. "Now, I wonder if it's stopped raining?"

She went over to the window and opened the blinds, saying, "Oh good, it has!" But then she suddenly looked really worried and cried, "Oh, dear me! Dear me!"

WHAT IS IT, MRS PARROT?

"It's Slasher!" said Mrs Parrot. "Er, I mean Mr Simpson. He's in our wildlife garden with his strimmer and shears! There's no telling what he'll do."

Slasher Simpson was just taking his shears to the beautiful butterfly bush we planted last month. But, as he did, something huge and greeny-brown, and *very*, *very* scaly began to slither out from behind it.

Mrs Parrot's eyes twinkled. "Oh, dear!" she said with a chuckle. "I think one of Eric's rainforest friends might be still about…"

"An anaconda, in fact!" said Mrs Parrot. "Probably the largest snake in the world. I'd say this one was a least ten metres long. They usually squeeze their victims to death then swallow them whole ... headfirst!"

At that moment Slasher Simpson saw the anaconda and turned the colour of the antpowder that's he's so fond of spreading around. A micro-second later he dropped his shears and began galloping across our playing fields!

"Obviously not a big fan of rainforest wildlife," laughed Mrs Parrot

"Unlike class 5M!" said Laxmi.

Which is how Mr Simpson got a lesson he'd never forget. And so did we!